A Don't-Get-Caught
# THE DOODLE NOTEBOOK

Written & Illustrated by
## Susan McBride

LARK BOOKS
A Division of Sterling Publishing Co., Inc.
New York

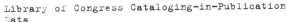

EDITOR:
Joe Rhatigan

ART DIRECTOR:
Susan McBride

ASSISTANT ART DIRECTOR:
Shannon Yokeley

PRODUCTION:
Celia Naranjo

ART INTERNS:
Chris Dollar
Brad Armstrong
Bradley Norris
Sarah House

Library of Congress Cataloging-in-Publication
Data

McBride, Susan (Susan A.), 1962-
   The don't-get-caught doodle notebook /
Susan McBride.
        p. cm.
   Includes index.
   ISBN 1-57990-702-4 (pbk.)
  1.  Doodles. 2.   Drawing--Technique. 3.
School notebooks.   I. Title.
NC915.D6M38 2005
741.2--dc22
                                    2005004466

10 9 8 7 6 5 4 3 2

Published by Lark Books, A Division of
Sterling Publishing Co., Inc.
387 Park Avenue South, New York, N.Y. 10016

Distributed in Canada by Sterling Publishing,
c/o Canadian Manda Group, 165 Dufferin Street
Toronto, Ontario, Canada M6K 3H6

Distributed in the United Kingdom by
GMC Distribution Services,
Castle Place, 166 High Street, Lewes,
East Sussex, England BN7 1XU

Distributed in Australia by
Capricorn Link (Australia) Pty Ltd.,
P.O. Box 704, Windsor, NSW 2756 Australia

If you have questions or comments about this
book, please contact:
Lark Books
67 Broadway
Asheville, NC 28801
(828) 253-0467

Manufactured in China

ISBN 13: 978-1-57990-702-0
ISBN 10: 1-57990-702-4

For information about custom editions,
special sales, premium and corporate
purchases, please contact Sterling
Special Sales Department at 800-805-5489
or specialsales@sterlingpub.com.

For Billy Beeler,
wherever you are...

# * Introduction

**H**ave you ever doodled your way to a week's worth of detention? Have you ever received the HAIRY EYEBALL from teachers and parents who think you're not paying attention because you're doodling? THE DON'T-GET-CAUGHT DOODLE NOTEBOOK is here to the rescue!

This mild-mannered, unassuming guide is disguised as an ordinary composition notebook. However, there's nothing ordinary about it. Packed inside you'll find everything you ever needed to doodle whenever you want—without getting caught.

In the first part of this book, flex your doodle muscles with simple yet strangely satisfying doodling techniques and drawing skills. You'll take scribbling to new heights. Learn the importance of the humble dot. And realize, with utter certainty, that crosshatching isn't just for chickens anymore.

In the second part of the book (which starts soon after the first part ends), aim your newly acquired arsenal of doodling skills at any animal, vegetable, or mineral that crosses your path. Draw your teachers (of course). Imagine future tattoos and where you'd put them.

Womp up a school lunch à la doodling. Contemplate grafitti. Finish a flip book. Draw what it feels like to be sick. Invent your own school mascot, and so much more.

In conclusion, the world would be lackluster without doodles and doodlers. In fact, many of the world's famous genius-types have doodled ideas, art, and amazing machines that have changed the world—usually for the better. (You can read about some of them in this book.) Go ahead and do the anti-boring study-hall activities found throughout. Draw and write your own stuff. Copy my stuff. Play the games. Change the world. But best of all DON'T GET CAUGHT!

Attention! Achtung! Atención!

Teacher about to snag you? Well, right in the middle of this book (located in the middle) are several pages of real fake notes. So, whenever you find yourself in a sticky situation due to doodling, flip to the center of the book and take a stab at looking studious. Teachers fall for it every time.

# Start with SCRIBBLES

Scribbling is just a long, continuous line overlapping and looping around. Get out a pen or pencil and give it a try.
IT IS WONDERFULLY SATISFYING.

Feel free to go
a little nuts!

# Scribbling can turn into almost anything...

# Scribbles make GREAT HAIR!

# Help these bald guys get some hair.

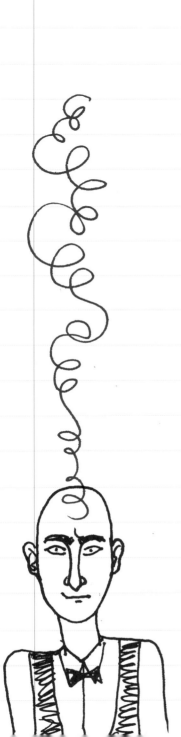

—Let's move on.

Roger!

# Historic Doodler
## Charles Darwin

hmmmm... Interesting Nesting Material..

hmmmm... Interesting Beak...

## NATURALIST DOODLER

### 1809-1882

Charles was a shy, confused young man. He was uncertain about what he wanted to be when he grew up. In 1831, he boarded a ship called HMS Beagle with lots of notebooks, and sailed to the Pacific coast of South America. For five years he studied wildlife and made notations and strange little sketches in his notebooks. The result of this study became his Theory of Evolution.

Still think doodling's for monkeys?

# Doodling and drawing come naturally to most creatures...

## Even chickens can draw.

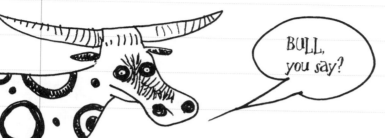

BULL,
you say?

Well, take a look and try it yourself. When chickens eat feed off the ground, they scratch with their feet and pointy beaks. They make little HATCH marks on the ground, and then they CROSS over them in their endless pursuit of lunch.

You can draw like a chicken. It's called CROSS-HATCHING. You can crosshatch designs or give form to line drawings (add shadow and shape).

I love the way you gave form to those line drawings.

Thanks, man. You gonna eat that?

Of course we HATCH, we're chickens!

You can make things look very dark or light, depending on the pressure you put on your pen or pencil and how many hatch marks you add.

Try it.

CROSS-HATCHING makes great shadows.

GALA
ORGANIC
9413 L

BANANO DE COSTA RICA
Quality

Make the hat higher, darling. More is more...

## Why do we draw it?

### COMPLICATED PATTERNS

Detailed, complex doodles may be a sign of an obsessive personality—an 'i' dotter and 't' crosser. They are often the weird little scribbles of introverts.

Extrovert

Introvert

If you can make
circles, you can draw
this centipede.

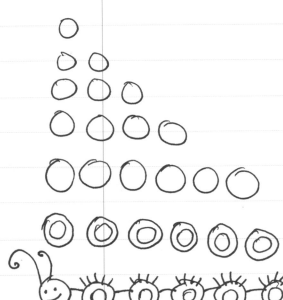

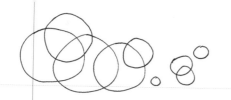

← the shouters

Technically,
these are
ovals.

# Circles

Finish the circle monster...

# evolve into different things...

### & the smaller
### they get,
### the closer
### to DOTS
they become..........

La La La, connect the dots!

Dots Incredible!

Dots are an important part of doodles, so don't forget about them—they can be eyeballs, dirt, nose holes, fleas, hairs.. .you name it.

Add dots

Add spots

Make
something
completely out
of dots.

The Princess & the Pea. Note: the pea is a dot.

# Historic Doodler

## Nikola Tesla

*tesla*

**ELECTRIFYING DOODLER**

## 1856-1943

Tesla was a Serbian-American scientist, electrical engineer, and inventor who helped lay the groundwork for modern electrical and communication systems. He was also a notebook keeper and doodler. After his death, his notebooks, private papers, and diaries revealed his true genius.

### AND He believed in aliens!

*greetings*

# Shading is Important

Shading an object gives it form and a sense of reality, if that's what you're after, artistically speaking...

It sure is!

...personally, I think reality is a
little overrated, but you should
definitely try it.

Flip it,
Flip it Good!

Pencils—especially soft graphite pencils—can give you a smudgy effect, which can look like real shadows. You can draw scribbles, crosshatch, draw a bunch of lines close together, or smear it all together to achieve this effect.

## Now YOU try it.

Draw a few simple shapes and add shadows and shade.

# Keep on the Sunny Side

Before we get too far
into shade, shadow,
and darkness, we
should talk about why
they exist.

The answer is: (Let there be) Light!

Ouch! I hate when
he does that! Who
does he think he is?

The dark
side of the Teddy Bear

The Light Source

The Teddy Bear

The way a light shines on the surface of an object determines where the shadows fall.

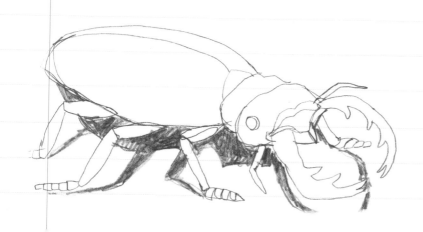

# Face it!

Easy tips on how to draw
a human face.

Start with an oval. Draw a
curved line down the center of
the oval. Make four lines
across the oval,
spaced approximately
as shown here.

1. The Eyebrow line
2. The Eyeball line
3. The Nose line
4. The Mouth line

The Eyebrow line
and the Nose line
show where the
ears usually go.

# Try it!

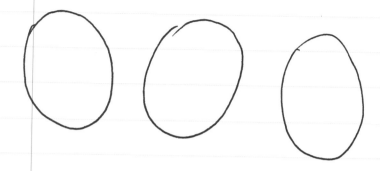

Oh dear!

# Now, look around at your fellow humans.

Most people don't exactly have oval-shaped heads. Some are round or oblong, angular or even peanut shaped. Also, their features are probably spaced a little differently. I call this CHARACTER.

# Add Special Features

Extraordinary Ears, Eyes, Noses, Warts, Glasses, Toupees,
Thin Lips, Large Gold Teeth, Scary lipstick, Frightening jewelry
...All these things give power and punch to your portraits.

Add a toupee

The EYES of
The Algebra Teacher

☐ Bad weekend

☐ Allergies

☐ Fight with wife

☐ Hates this class

☐ All of the above

# Class! Let us apply what we have learned about Doodling.

## It's Time to Draw Your Teacher

**1** OK, here's the deal: get caught doing this and you FRY.

**2** Now, relax. Try not to stare directly at your subject...that would be your teacher. Draw quickly, don't get bogged down in details, let it flow...

**3** Emphasize the obvious... does your teacher have really hairy eyebrows, freakishly small ears, a tragic sense of style? Start there. Your drawing does not have to be perfect—you just need to get the point across.

Note: Success in drawing teachers could win you a strange kind of fame with your classmates.

# Why do we draw it?

Eye doodles may mean the
doodler is slightly paranoid—
thinking Big Brother is
always watching...

# Go ahead—Draw your teacher*

*A Word to the Wise—remember the fake class notes in the center of this book? Mark those pages! A quick flip to the center of this notebook could save you some trouble.

## The HAIR of
## The English Literature Teacher

- ☐ Thinks she's Lady MacBeth
- ☐ Washes her hair in glue
- ☐ Keeps Rats
- ☐ Oblivious

# What's REALLY going on in the Teacher's Lounge?

zzzzz Z zZ zzzzz Z z

DRAW your own conclusions.

# Frida Kahlo

## FLAMBOYANT DOODLER

## 1907-1951

When Frida was 18, she was
in a terrible bus accident
that nearly killed her. In the
hospital, she began to paint
(on her body cast), draw, and
keep sketchbooks. She often
painted herself dressed in the
colorful, traditional costumes
of her homeland, Mexico. Her
numerous visual diaries tell
the story of her WILD life.
(She probably drove her parents
crazy!) She loved animals and
had a pet fawn and a hairless
dog named Señor Xólotl.

# Neatness counts?

What does your

## penmanship

look like?

Teachers preach NEATNESS because they have to stay up all night reading your papers.

What's HER Problem?

In REAL LIFE, people don't spend a lot of time worrying about this stuff.

Rx

Date

Inez needs lots of R8 R+ no candy!

← See what I mean?

Doctors have CRUMMY handwriting. They're busy saving lives and filing insurance papers. There's no time for good penmanship! If you're considering becoming a doc, start loosening your handwriting standards right about now.

Yes, Ladies and gents, writing your name over and over (or your future married name, girls) IS a form of doodling.

If you go into finance, chances are you'll sign lots of checks.

Develop a quick, authoritative signature—$OMETHING that $UGGE$T$ POWER. You'll also want to invest in a really expensive pen.

A time-honored typeface, great for posters.

BALLOON LETTERS

# Morse Code

If you can find a geeky friend to learn this with you, you have it made. Nobody will know what you are talking about!

A •—    B —•••    C —•—•    D —••

E •    F ••—•    G ——•    H ••••

I ••    J •———    K —•—    L •—••

M ——    N —•    O ———    P •——•

Q ——•—    R •—•    S •••    T —

U ••—    V •••—    W •——

X —••—    Y —•——    Z ——••

•—•—•—

## Full Stop

••• ——— •••

## S O S

FAKE CLASS NOTES
start on the
next page.

# Language arts     Thursday 2/19

Have to
on/o/mat/o/poe/ia  ⟵ Spell it too-on test
formation of a word that sounds like
what it is: BUZZ, CRACK, (MURMUR)-spelling word
* for homework give 5 examples - find 5
in spelling words, AND

moan
✓groan  ⟵ Take these words
scream   and write ③ sentences, or small
whoosh   paragraphs *Extra credit-do ⑤ sentences.
clang
✓swoop   1. My sister moaned and groaned
✓drip       because she had a scrape on
✓splash     her leg.
weep
✓scrape   2. Miss Hutchinson swooped down on
gurgle      Jim, because he did'nt do his homework,
crunch      which caused him to weep.

           3. The splash AND drip of the sink
              caused the woman to
              scream.

# Spelling Words

| | | |
|---|---|---|
| abandon | tendency | incurred |
| accidental | survival | occuring |
| acceptance | affidavit | admitting |
| alligator | consolidate | overlapping |
| controller | gratitude | artificial |
| commemorate | undoubtedly | investor |
| dismal | appetite | ancestors |
| corrupt | curiosity | particular |
| junior | guardian | murmur |
| patrolled | saturate | vinegar |
| exposure | voluntary | necessity |
| integral | barbeque | saturate |
| immigration | dominate | conqueror |
| incubator | hysterical | |
| forbidden | immense | |
| ornament | imposter | |
| recital | permitted | |

# Pythagorean Theorum

*Test on Thursday

$$\sqrt{a^2 + b^2}$$

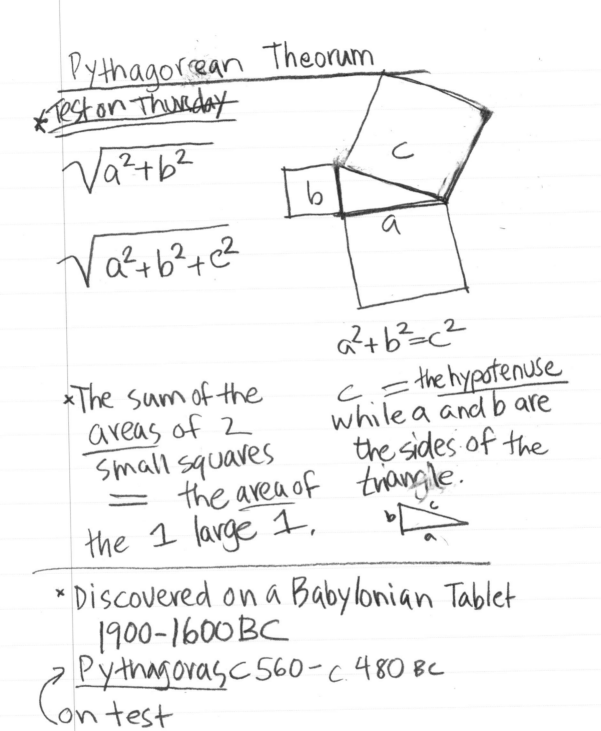

$$\sqrt{a^2 + b^2 + c^2}$$

$$a^2 + b^2 = c^2$$

*The sum of the areas of 2 small squares = the area of the 1 large 1.

$c$ = the hypotenuse while $a$ and $b$ are the sides of the triangle.

* Discovered on a Babylonian Tablet 1900-1600 BC

> Pythagoras c 560 - c. 480 BC

on test

* Bring Protactor + calculator
   #2 pencil + eraser

2D to 3D, the formula for the diagonal of shape built on orthogonal segments remained the same * Except #of terms 2 to 3 (3D) - But both cases _Squared was segmented

All 3 edges come from one of the vertices + are perpendicular to each other,

$$A = qr/2 \quad B = rp/2, \quad c = p^q/2$$

$\times$ Show that $A^2 + B^2 + c^2 = D^2$

$$D = ha/2$$
$$h^2 = K^2 + p^2$$
AND $aK/2$

$$4D^2 = a^2 h^2$$
$$= a^2 (K^2 + p^2)$$
$$= 4A^2 + a^2 p^2$$
$$= 4A^2 + (rp^2 + a^2)$$
$$= 4A^2 + (rp)^2 + (ca)^2$$
$$= 4A^2 + 4B^2 + 4C^2$$

# smile

People who dot Is with smiley faces,
hearts, and big circles are:

☐ Trying out for cheerleading

☐ Squealers, as a form of greeting

☐ Afraid of bugs

☐ Fond of photos of kittens

☐ all of the above

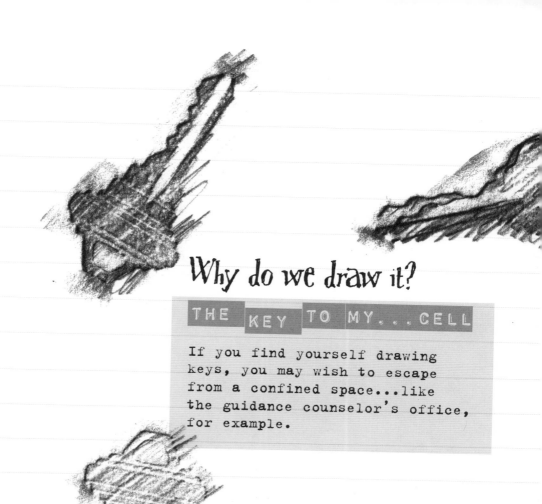

# Why do we draw it?

## THE KEY TO MY...CELL

If you find yourself drawing keys, you may wish to escape from a confined space...like the guidance counselor's office, for example.

Squirrels use their tails to communicate messages.

# Leonardo da Vinci

I'll have the veggie plate, grazie!

## RENAISSANCE DOODLER

## 1452-1519

Leonardo was an Italian Renaissance
man: a scientist, an inventor,
a sculptor, and a painter. His most
famous painting is the Mona Lisa.
After his death, his numerous secret
sketchbooks were found, which
revealed drawings and notes on ideas
for airplanes, tanks, submarines,
elevators, and parachutes! It took
the rest of the world 400 years to
catch up. Eccentric and secretive,
he wrote backwards in his sketchbooks. A mirror was needed to
read them.

He was also
a vegetarian.

NO M.S.G.

SOY SAUCE

GREDIENTS: WATER, SALT,
EGETABLE PROTEIN, CORN
RUP, CARAMEL COLOR,
10 OF 1% SODIUM BENZOATE

.Y. INDUSTRIES, INC.
2500 SECAUCUS, RD.
RTH BERGEN, NJ 07047

It's your turn to FLIP IT!
But first turn toward the end of
the notebook to see what happens.

Tuna Surprise!

GROAN...

Womp up the lunch you are craving...
à la doodling...

Tired of the lame lunchbox
your aunt gave you?
Design the one you REALLY want,
right here, right now.

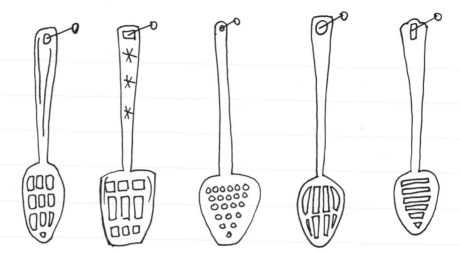

The Lunch Lady Slotted Spoon Hall of Fame

# So, you think you want a Tattoo?

Whadd'a ya lookin' at, kid?

Used to be, the only folks who had tattoos were creepy old sailors.

Darlink, give Nana a kiss.

Nowadays all kinds of people have them—even grandmothers!

If your parents are not keen on the subject of TATTOOS, don't be sad. Nothing is stopping you from designing one (even if you can't get it RIGHT NOW).

A tattoo should say something about you...

Where would you put a TATTOO?

# Why do we draw it?

## LUXURY AUTOMOBILES

Drawing DELUXE cars usually shows
a desire for material goods, like
a killer stereo, and excellent
speakers, and custom wheels, and a
wicked paint job, and...

Dude!

## DOGMATIC DOODLER

# 1905-1982

Born Alice Rosenbaum, she lived
through the Russian Revolution,
then changed her name to AYN
(rythmes with "mine") and, rumor
has it, she took the last name,
Rand, from her typewriter. Ayn Rand
became a novelist and philosopher.
She scribbled in notebooks as a
young person and continued on
throughout her life. She was a
person of extreme ideas and
notions. The effects of her fiction
and philosophy on people are
equally extreme.

You're not lookin' so hot...

# Have you ever been SICK AT SCHOOL?

MOM, that lady's legs are on upside down!

Our Lady of Perpetual Embarrassment, Mrs. Murphy.

I'm here to pick up Michael.

What took you so long?

School Nurse

MOM! I PUKED in GYM!

poo poo

Draw what it feels like to be sick.

Nothing gets the blood flowing faster than a dodgeball to the face!

# P.E.*

Coach Swinehund,
also "teaches" Health

* Public Embarrassment?

# Excuses for getting out of

1  I forgot my gym shoes.

2  I have a communicable fungal infection.

3  I am recovering from a terrible wedgie.

4  I have a medical condition that prevents me from undressing in front of other people.

5  The Salisbury steak at lunch did not agree with me.

Keep going...

How much can you lift?

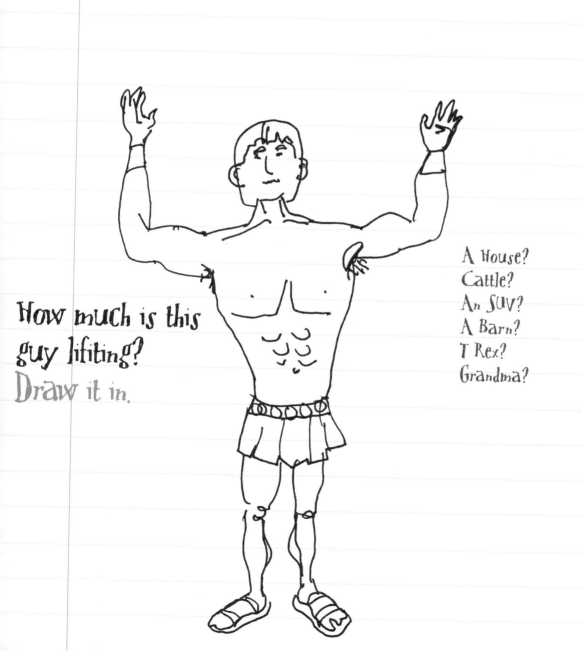

How much is this guy lifting? Draw it in.

A House?
Cattle?
An SUV?
A Barn?
T Rex?
Grandma?

If you are not athletically inclined but love sports, consider being a MASCOT.

Invent your own Mascot.

# Why do we draw it?

Repeatedly drawing arrows and
pointy objects may be an indication
of extreme ambition.

# Graffiti is Old News

*Think you've invented something new in graffiti?* THINK AGAIN.

It has been around for ages. "Beware of Dog" was scrawled on the walls of ancient Rome, along with all kinds of other things.

"CAVE CANEM*"

FERNANDO MAKES GREAT PIZZA

\* Beware of this Dog?

YOUR
MOTHER
HAS A
MOUSTACHE

# KILROY
# WAS
# HERE

Kilroy showed up during
World War II, when the
American military traveled
abroad. He was drawn on
everything— airplanes,
bombs, ships, even latrines.

Graffiti is recognized as ART in some parts of the world.

It speaks to my sense of angst.

Textural!
Stunning!

ZORO

FLE

# Where would you put graffiti, and what style would you choose?

A Warning?
A Proclamation of LOVE?
A Political Message?
Public Announcement?
Religious Info?
Promoting your Favorite Band?
A Secret Symbol?

# To Graffiti or NOT to Graffiti ?

Defacing public and private property is definitely illegal.
So if you choose TO anyway—consider yourself warned, dude.

Give Peace a Chance.

# Historic Doodler
# John Lennon

ROCK-N-ROLL

DOODLER 1940-1980

The coolest member of
The Beatles, John was
unconventional and witty.
He kept sketchbooks and
notebooks throughout his
life. His drawing style was
wild. Controversial and
often in the news for
speaking his truth,
he was beloved by his
many fans.

Voilà!

Write a caption.

# Why do we draw it?

## TANGLED WEB WE WEAVE

Drawing webs can symbolize a sense
of entrapment, or a desire to
draw someone into a particular
situation (like your prom date?).

I am like so glad your grandmother's house-keeper knows my mother's sister and we could arrange to go to the prom together! This is going to be like sooo fun! I have EVERYTHING planned...

# Historic Doodler

## Hildegard von Bingen

### 1098-1179

Hildegard was a nun who was INSPIRED FROM ABOVE. Ultimately a visionary writer, composer, and botanist, she began life as a sickly, weird little kid. Her family actually gave her away to the church. Headachy and fearful, she refused to write down her thoughts and visions. Her teachers recognized her talents and provided her with a monk to write and draw for her. (Not a bad deal!)

# Why do we draw it?
## GIMME SHELTER

If you are drawing lots of
umbrellas, you may wish to
provide help to a loved one.

Sometimes you have to be your own Superhero.

I'm tired. YOU finish this...

# Acknowledgments

I am grateful to the people at Lark Books for this opportunity. Thank you, Celia, for asking me to consider this project. It has been a pleasure to bounce ideas off Joe, and also to discuss music.

To my good friends and family, past and present, who have encouraged me to find my own way—thank you: Father McBride, Dolly-Dear, Christine & Fernando, Mike & Ruthie, Annie, Lorrene, Megan, Fairy-god-mother-Heather, Sista Theresa, Flavo-Rich, Robert-O, Dr. H., and the Saltmice. Thank you, Karl Galloway for looking the book over and giving great suggestions.

Michael & Margaret Rose, I thank my lucky stars that you are in my life. For endless inspiration—Nathan, Bella, & Luna, you are the best.